T5-BAV-398

Valerie B. Hird

Valerie B. Hird

Anatolian Journeys
A memoir

Nohra Haime Gallery Editions

Design: Paola Gribaudo
© 1995, Nohra Haime Gallery Editions
ISBN: 1-886125-01-5
Library of Congress Catalogue Card Number: 94-74004

Anatolian Journeys
A memoir

I was in central Anatolia when I recalled the childhood images from my National Geographic magazines. The stories of explorers who had just traversed the North Pole, or had been accepted by tribes of roaming African Masai, had a narcotic effect on me and left me feverish with adolescent schemes.

When I arrived in Turkey, I had the same feeling. I was assailed on all levels, not only by new people and places, but also aesthetically. The physical landscape combined with the textiles, which were everywhere, created such an artistic frenzy within me that I felt the need to withdraw into a dark, empty room each night. Since there were none available, I ended up being buffeted by images I could not hope to assimilate.

I was able to find my way into the mountains above the Aegean Sea with the help of some rug dealers. I spent two extraordinary days in a car with clenched sphincter muscles —to the accompaniment of Liszt's Hungarian Rhapsodies — as we careened over the steep mountain roads. I drank raki

and cay with the local fathers, photographed women weaving and spinning, watched a soccer match and even took
an interesting diversion to an insane asylum, the reason for
which I could never determine.

The whole series of events were, of course, dictated,
shaped and ultimately toasted by endless negotiations with
the guide, the driver and a whole procession of bystanders.

I arrived on the central Anatolian Steppe to find a
breathtaking landscape from another planet. Under the spell
of this lunar terrain, I explored the region and its people;
many of whom still live in the caves hollowed out by their
ancestors. I hooked up with an American man, we rented
mountain bikes and pressed on into places known only to
locals, land tortoises, feral cats and desert hawks.

The difficulty in travelling as we did was that there were
no maps. We relied on rough line drawings provided by
enthusiastic but unintelligible tour outfits, and on my crash
course in "Diplomatic Turkish". We reached one village in

time to have a lunch which was supervised by the entire male population. The women were working in the fields. Pointing to our "map", I asked directions to a nearby village. Everyone smiled, shook their heads and made walking motions with their fingers. In my innocence, I assumed they were underestimating our cycling ability. We got a mile out of town when we lost the road. Hailing a passing tractor, I determined there was no road, not even a path. Just a general direction. It was a lesson in local knowledge underlined as the village turned out to wave to us as we passed back through.

With few exceptions, I never got a good night's sleep or a hot shower. But in the succeeding months — surrounded by the little daily luxuries of my life — images of an extraordinary adventure began to emerge.

Valerie B. Hird

Kurdish Landscape II

Southern Marshes Kilim Runner

Sunrise Morning

Study, Tribal Landscape I

Study, Tribal Landscape IV

Study, Tribal Landscape III

Study, Tribal Landscape II

Fairy Chimneys Illhara Valley

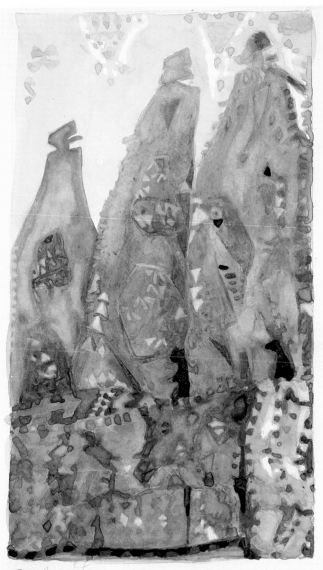

FAIRY CHIMNEYS
IHLARA VALLEY

21

Amulet, Kilim and House

ANGULAR MOTIFS + HOUSE, MANISA, WINTER ENCAMPMENT

23

Souk, Istanbul

Your, Istanbul   5/93

Manisa Weavers

MANISA-WEAVERS

Rug Dealer, Ismir

RUG DEALER IZMIR   5/93

Manisa Weaver

MANISA WEAVER MOTHER

Interior, Manisa

INTERIOR, MANISA

33

Mother, Daughter, Manisa

MY HOSTESS   MOTHER DAUGHTER MANISA

Weaving Room, Manisa

37

Urgup Women Knitting

URGÜP WOMEN KNITTING   9410

Digging Vegetables

Digging Vegetables Near Istanbul

41

Washing Manisa

Fisherman, Bosporus

FISHERMAN AT THE BOSPORUS

Somewhere in The Souk, Istanbul

Somewhere in the Souk, Istanbul   5/93

47

Manisa Kilim

49

Southern Marshes

SOUTHERN MARSHES

Illhara Kilim

ILLIARA KILIM

53

Kurdish Kandscape I

Valerie B. Hird was born in a small town near Springfield, Massachusetts, on July 6, 1955 with as she says, "a number two pencil in her hand". Life in Massachusetts was basically quiet and orderly. Her father, a lawyer, and her mother, originally from New York City, were enamored by the work of Andrew Wyeth; and as a child, Hird copied that artist's style diligently. She was proficient enough to have her first one-person show at the age of sixteen.

Her paternal gradparents, however were inveterate travellers and collectors. Their home in Plainfield, New Jersey, was filled with everything from aboriginal masks to oriental objects. "They never threw anything out, lived to 96, and left behind a lifetime of souvenirs from around the world. By the time they died, everything had become an antique".

Her maternal grandmother — the editor-in-chief of Mademoiselle magazine — was also addicted to collecting: textiles, shoes, fans, tapestries and ceremonial robes from any century and any country. "She wasn't a scholar, but she had wonderful intuition and exquisite taste".

It was her yearly trips to her grandparents where her interest in rugs and textiles developed as well as a pleasure in chaos. She remembers these visits as being second-hand travels to a different universe.

At the age of eighteen, Hird enrolled at Beloit College in Wisconsin where whe chose to major in archeology in the hopes of becoming an archeological illustrator. Her first 'dig' in Panama cured her of that ambition forever. "I did hundreds of sketches of rocks that "might" have been touched by pre-historic man. But there was no creative thought to the work, no artistry".

She then transferred to The Rhode Island School of Design, where she found her true passion: painting. After her first year there, a painting.instructor whom she admired told her: "This isn't working. Either drop out or break your fingers". It was only then that she began to turn away from New England realism and toward a wider heritage she'd unconsciously absorbed as a child.

While at the Rhode Island School of Design, Hird also apprenticed to a group that did specialty framing and restoration. She found restoration to be particularly satisfying; "an art form that has its own absorbing challenges". Working in addition as an assistant to the chief curator at the Museum, Hird became a conservator who catalogued, prepared and installed museum exhibitions. "It was crazy. I was holding down three jobs, and at the same time doing fifty different versions of the same painting for one of my professors. I didn't know what I loved more".

After graduating in 1978 and bicycling through England, Wales and the Netherlands with her new husband, Hird moved to Burlington, Vermont, where she opened a gallery called Passepartout, dedicated to the new Vermont artists. During the ensuing years, she painted, managed the gallery, did restoration, and ran an art consulting service for corporations and institutions.

In 1986, divorced and with an infant son to support, Hird decided to focus exclusively on painting and on motherhood. "I was also having recurring dreams about travel".

The dreams became reality when, in 1987, she went to Andalusian Spain for the first time and became mesmerized by the landscape and by the ghosts of the Moors. After a summer spent studying in London, she returned to Spain two years later and was introduced to the Royal Tapestry Workshop in Madrid which she haunted until going back to the Andalusian countryside between Jerez de la Frontera and Zahara. "I left part of my heart there".

Since then, Hird has been able to spend some portions of each year back-packing to new places. She has explored the Nile Valley in Egypt, the highlands and the rocky inlets of Scotland, and the Anatolian plateau in Turkey. She next plans to visit the Black Sea coastline of Turkey, Castillian and Salamancan Spain, and Latin America, beginning with Cartagena. Her son Blackwell (a family name) has become an avid rock climber and shell searcher, and accompanies her on the easier journeys.

The world for Hird is a tapestry of light, hues and textures that echo ancient and immutable patterns of human life. These are reflected in her oil paintings. Each of her journeys also gives birth to a new series of associations and memories in the form of watercolors.

These are the memoirs from her last trip to Turkey.